Don't Make a Sound

By Mary Packard
Illustrations by Lane Yerkes

Gareth Stevens Publishing
A WORLD ALMANAC EDUCATION GROUP COMPANY

Please visit our web site at: www.garethstevens.com
For a free color catalog describing Gareth Stevens Publishing's
list of high-quality books and multimedia programs,
call 1-800-542-2595 (USA) or 1-800-387-3178 (Canada).
Gareth Stevens Publishing's fax: (414) 332-3567.

Library of Congress Cataloging-in-Publication Data

Packard, Mary.
　　　Don't make a sound / by Mary Packard; illustrated by Lane Yerkes.
　　　　　p. cm.
　　　Summary: When Bunny gets home from school his little brothers and sisters
　　are napping, so he is very "quiet."
　　　　ISBN 0-8368-4099-2 (lib. bdg.)
　　　　[1. Noise—Fiction. 2. Naps (Sleep)—Fiction. 3. Brothers and sisters—Fiction.
　　4. Rabbits—Fiction.] I. Title: Do not make a sound. II. Yerkes, Lane, ill. III. Title.
　　PZ7.P1247Do　　2004
　　[E]—dc22　　　　　　　　　　　　　　　　　　　　　　　　　　2003059211

First published in 2004 by
Gareth Stevens Publishing
A World Almanac Education Group Company
330 West Olive Street, Suite 100
Milwaukee, Wisconsin 53212 USA

Gareth Stevens editor: Barbara Kiely Miller
Gareth Stevens art direction: Tammy Gruenewald

Printed in the United States of America

1 2 3 4 5 6 7 8 9 08 07 06 05 04

When I get home from school, Mommy always says, "Shhh! You must be quiet as a mouse because your little brothers and sisters are napping."

"I will," I whisper, but sometimes the door makes a teeny-tiny sound when I close it. "Oops," I say.

3

"I'll tiptoe upstairs to wash
for lunch, Mommy."

I can reach the faucet all by myself.
I never forget to flush the toilet.

When I'm done, I always remember to close the door.

"Hooray! Spaghetti for lunch! Let me help."

It's a good thing I know how to use the vacuum cleaner.

VROOOOOOOOM!

Mommy said I should just go play. I think
I'll play my drums. My teacher always says,
"Practice makes perfect."

Mommy said I have to play outside now.
That's all right. I'll go for a ride on my train.

I wonder if the babies are still sleeping. Oops!
The door is stuck. I'll just ring the bell.

"Sorry, Mommy," I say.

"Go to your room," Mommy says. "You must be quiet!"

"Okay," I tell her, but it's not fair. I didn't slam the door on purpose.

11

WHOOP! WHOOP! RRRRROOOWWW!

I have to find a quiet toy. I know! My fire truck's not too noisy! I'll go show Mommy.

Uh-oh! Mommy made a big noise!

Mommy woke up the babies, but that's okay.
She's lucky she has me around to help take
care of them.

About the Author

Mary Packard has been writing children's books for as long as she can remember. Packard lives in Northport, New York, with her family. Besides writing, she loves music, theater, animals, and of course, children of all ages.

About the Illustrator

Lane Yerkes graduated from the Philadelphia College of Art and served four years in the U.S. Navy. He has illustrated children's books, textbooks, and magazine and newspaper articles, as well as created fabric designs, posters, and logos. Yerkes lives on the southwest coast of Florida, not far from the Everglades.

BANG!

ACHOO!

CLANG CLANG!

THUMP

BING!

THUMP!

BONG!

THUMP!

SWOOOOSH!

CLASH!

BOOM!

TAPPITY TAP!

CRASH!

BANG!